MW01144452

FRENCH RECIPES

By Mattie Clement

This booklet is going to provide you the most delicious French recipes that are easy to make and tasty to eat. So, pack yourself up and let's jump into the ocean of Deliciousness with rich flavors and spices!

FRENCH TOAST STICKS

Ingredients:

- ✓ Almond milk   1 cup
- ✓ Vanilla extract   1 tsp
- ✓ Cinnamon, grounded   1 tsp
- ✓ Sandwich bread   8 slices
- ✓ Granulated sugar   2 tsp
- ✓ Butter
- ✓ Eggs   2
- ✓ Salt to taste

Instructions:

i. In a bowl, whisk together eggs, milk, salt, vanilla, and cinnamon. Then spread over a baking dish. Cut the bread into thirds and place a few at a time into the egg mixture and flip to make sure both sides of bread are well-coated.

ii. Now coat the bread pieces with granulated sugar from both sides.

iii. In a large skillet, melt butter on medium flame.

iv. Cook the bread sticks in skillet for about 3-5 minutes until golden browned and crispy.

v.   Your French toast sticks are ready, enjoy!

Time Required:

- Preparation Time   20mins
- Cook Time   20mins
- Total Time   40mins

BASQUE BRAISED CHICKEN WITH PEPPERS

Ingredients

- 3 tbsp. extra-virgin olive oil

- 4 small fresh chorizo sausages
- 4 skin-on, boneless chicken breasts (about 8 oz. each), halved crosswise
- Kosher salt
- 6 sprigs thyme
- 2 large garlic cloves, lightly crushed
- 1 bay leaf
- 1 yellow onion
- 1 shallot
- 1 tomato, diced (3/4 cup)
- 2 tbsp. tomato paste
- 1 cup chicken stock
- 1 1/2 cups dry white wine
- 10 jarred piquillo peppers, drained
- 12 boiled small new potatoes
- 1/4 cup green apple, finely diced
- 2 tbsp. chopped flat-leaf parsley, for garnish
- 2 tsp. piment d'Espelette

Instructions

1. Preheat oven to 450 °. Meanwhile, in an 8 quart Dutch oven or large, high-sided cast iron skeleton, heat 1 tablespoon oil over medium heat. Add the sauce and cook, stirring occasionally, until browned, about 8-8 minutes. Transfer the sausage to a large plate, cut into 3-inch pieces and set aside. Put the remaining oil in the pot and increase the heat. Season the chicken all season with salt and pepper, then add to the skin in the pan. Take thyme asparagus, garlic and bay leaves between the pieces. Cook until shiny, 5-7 minutes. Transfer the chicken, thyme, garlic, and bay leaf to a plate with the sauce.

2. In the same pot over medium heat, add onions and sauerkraut and cook, stirring occasionally, for about 5 minutes. Stir in tomatoes and cook for 3 minutes, until

liquid evaporates. Add tomato paste and cook for 1 minute, stirring. Scrape the brown bits from the bottom of the pan, stir in 1-2 cups of stock and 1-2 teaspoons of salt. Cook until most of the liquid has evaporated, 5-8 minutes. Return the thyme, garlic, bay leaf, sausages, and chicken (to the skin) to the pot. Transfer to the oven and fry until the chicken is cooked through, about 10 minutes. Transfer the chicken and sauce to a plate.

3. Place the pot over medium-high heat. Add the wine, paprika, and the remaining 1 cup of stock and bring to a boil. Cook, stirring occasionally, until the liquid is half full, about 10 minutes. Remove from heat. Add chicken and sauce, and potatoes (or serve them) if desired. Sprinkle with apples,

parsley, and piment d'Espelette and serve directly from the pot or on a plate.

BARIGOULE OF SPRING VEGETABLES

Ingredients

- Kosher salt and black pepper, to taste
- 4 oz. snow peas, trimmed
- 1⁄3 cup fresh peas
- 6 baby carrots with green tops, carrots peeled and halved lengthwise
- 1 bunch pencil asparagus
- 1⁄2 tsp. coriander seeds
- 1⁄4 cup plus 1 Tbsp. olive oil
- 10 cloves garlic, peeled and smashed
- 4 bulbs baby fennel, trimmed and halved, or 2 medium fennel, quartered

- 4 bulbs spring onions, greens thinly sliced, white onions peeled leaving stem end trimmed and attached, and halved
- 4 cups vegetable stock
- 10 sprigs thyme
- 5 whole black peppercorns
- 1 bay leaf
- 1 vanilla bean, split lengthwise
- 3 tbsp. sherry vinegar
- Cilantro sprigs, for garnish
- Maldon flake sea salt, for garnish

Instructions

1. Bring 6 kW. A boiling brine saucepan. While working in batches, cook ice peas, peas, carrots and asparagus until crispy tender, about 1 minute for peas, and 2-3 minutes for carrots and asparagus. Transfer the vegetables to an ice bath until cool. Throw, discard the rubber band from the asparagus, and set aside.
2. Pleasant, clean the pan for 1-2 minutes and wipe the toasted coriander seeds over

medium height. Add 1/4 cup oil. Cook the garlic until golden, --— minutes, and, using a spoon, transfer to a bowl. Cook fennel and white onion for 6-2 minutes. Transfer to a bowl with garlic. Add chopped onion greens, stock, thyme, pepper, bay leaf, and vanilla bean. Do not reduce until half, about 30 minutes. Pressure back in stock and pan; add the remaining oil, vinegar, salt and pepper and heat in the middle. Stir in all preserved vegetables; Cook, cover, and heat the vegetables for minutes. Divide the vegetables between the cups and the stomach on top. Garnish with greedy asparagus and sea salt.

ALSATIAN BACON AND ONION TART (TARTE FLAMBÉE)

Ingredients:

- 1/2 cup crème fraîche
- 1 cup fromage blanc or cream cheese at room temperature

- 1⁄8 tsp. nutmeg, freshly grated
- 1 tsp. kosher salt, plus more to taste
- Freshly ground white pepper, to taste
- 1 3⁄4 cups flour, plus more for dusting
- 1 tsp. baking powder
- 3 tbsp. olive oil
- 2 egg yolks
- 8 strips smoked bacon, finely chopped
- 1 medium white onion, thinly sliced

Instructions

1. Preheat an oven to 500 in which the pizza stone is placed on the center rack. In a bowl, mix cream frames, frothy blanks, nutmeg, and salt and white pepper. Sit on one side.

2. Knead flour, baking powder, and 1 tbsp. Salt in a bowl. Make a well in the middle. In another bowl, add whisking oil, eucalyptus, and 1-2 cups of water and mix well. Using a fork, stir until a loose dough is formed. Turn to a light surface. Knead the dough for 1 minute. Divide the flour into 3 pieces. Work

with 1 piece of flour at a time, put in a 12 " circle, and place on a baking sheet on parchment paper. Spread 1⁄2 cup cheese mixture in a circle, leaving 1-22 borders around one corner. Sprinkle with a little bacon and onion. Transfer the dough (on parchment paper) to the pizza stone. Bake for 8-10 minutes, lightly browned and crispy. Repeat.

APPLE-CINNAMON BOSTOCK

Ingredients:

For the frangipane:

- 1 cup sliced almonds
- 1⁄2 cup sugar
- 2 large eggs
- 1 stick unsalted butter (4 oz.), softened slightly
- 1⁄2 tsp. kosher salt
- 1 tsp. pure vanilla extract

- 1 tbsp. Calvados or spiced rum

For the toasts:

- Nonstick spray
- 6 (1-inch-thick) slices milk bread, brioche, or another good-quality, enriched white bread, lightly toasted
- 1⁄4 cup plus 2 Tbsp. prepared cinnamon syrup
- 1⁄4 cup plus 2 Tbsp. apple butter (homemade or store-bought)
- 1 1⁄3 cups sliced almonds
- Powdered sugar, for serving

Instructions

1. Make foreign drinks: In a food processor, add 1 cup almonds, sugar and lentils and grind finely. Add eggs, butter, and salt to a smooth paste, and stir. Drizzle to add drizzle in vanilla and calados .. Transfer the mixture to a bowl and let cool for 30 minutes or overnight.

2. Place a rack in the center of the oven and preheat to 375. Cover a large baking sheet with baking sheet and lightly oil the paper with a non-stick spray. Place the toasts on a baking sheet and brush freely with cinnamon syrup on both sides. Spread each piece aside with 1 tablespoon apple butter followed by a cup of almond paste.
3. Place the remaining 1-1 cups of chopped almonds in a shallow dish. Press the prepared toasts into the almond dish to coat the fringepan side with the almonds. Transfer toasts to almond side up, baking sheet.
4. Cook until the almonds are golden and the frying pan is slightly cracked and set but still soft, 18-20 minutes. Serve with powdered sugar, warm or at room temperature.

BASQUE-STYLE FISH WITH GREEN PEPPERS AND MANILA CLAMS

Ingredients:

- 1/3 cup extra-virgin olive oil
- 2 cloves garlic, finely minced (1 Tbsp.)
- 1 tbsp. all-purpose flour
- 1/2 cup dry white wine
- 2 cups fish stock or clam broth
- 3/4 tsp. kosher salt, or more to taste
- 1 lb. assorted mild green peppers cut into 1/4-inch strips
- 1 medium Spanish onion, thinly sliced
- 2 tbsp. chopped fresh flat-leaf parsley, plus more for garnish
- 2 lb. skin-on, boneless hake, striped bass, or haddock, cut into 8 equal fillets
- 12 Manila clams, scrubbed
- 1-2 tsp. piment d'Espelette

Instructions

1. In a 12-inch skewer, heat the olive oil over medium heat. Add garlic and cook, stirring occasionally, until just 1 minute, brown. Sprinkle flour over garlic and stir to collect. Add the wine and cook, stirring rapidly, until the mixture thickens and thickens slightly, approx. 2 minutes Add the fish stock and kosher salt, then bring the mixture back to a boil. Add pepper, onion and parsley, and spread evenly on the bottom of the pan. Raise the heat to high, cover the pan, and boil until the vegetables are tender, about 5 minutes.

2. Uncover the pan and place the skin of the fish pieces in a single layer on top of the vegetables. Settle the words between the fish with the salt of the flats and season with salt. Cover and cook until the fillets in the center just become opaque and the word opens, 5-7 minutes. (Do not delete any words that do not open.)

3. On a deep serving platter, scatter the vegetables, then place the fish and kalam

on top. Spoon the remaining broth over the fish and garnish with chopped parsley and asparagus pepper, if used; Serve immediately.

STEAK DIANE

Ingredients:

- 2 tbsp. canola oil
- 4 (4 oz.) filet mignon steaks
- 1 1/2 cups beef stock
- 2 tbsp. unsalted butter
- 2 cloves garlic, minced
- 1 shallot, minced
- 4 oz. oyster or hen-of-the-woods mushrooms, torn into small pieces
- 1/4 cup cognac or brandy
- 1/4 cup heavy cream
- 1 tbsp. Dijon mustard
- 1 tbsp. Worcestershire sauce

- 1/4 tsp. hot sauce, such as Tabasco
- 1 tbsp. minced parsley
- 1 tbsp. minced chives
- Kosher salt and freshly ground black pepper, to taste

Instructions

1. Heat oil in a 12 " scallet over medium-high heat. Season with salt and pepper, and add to the skeleton. For medium rare, lightly fry once, about 4 to 5 minutes, until browned on both sides and cooked to desired texture. Transfer the stacks to a plate, and set aside.
2. Return the skeleton to high heat, and add the stock; Until 1-2 cups, reduce to 10 minutes. Pour into a bowl, and set aside. Return the skeleton to the heat, and add the butter; Add garlic and cloves, and stir, stirring, for about 2 minutes. Add the mushrooms, and cook, stirring, until they release a liquid and these vapors and mushrooms turn brown, about 2 minutes.

Add kongak and light to match with light.
Cook until the flame dies. Stir in the typical
stock, cream, daisy, Worcestershire and hot
sauce, and then return the stalks to the
scale. Cook, turning into sauce, until hot
and the sauce thickens, about 4 minutes.
Place the steak on a plate and add the
parsley and chives to the sauce. Pour the
sauce over the steaks to serve.

FRENCH BANH MI

Ingredients:

- Leftover raw veggies   (150g)
- Vegan white wine vinegar   (3 tbsp)
- Golden caster sugar   (1 tbsp)
- French baguette   (1 long)
- Hummus   (100g)
- Finely sliced cooked tempeh   (175g)
- ½ small pack coriander   (to serve)
- ½ small pack mint leaves   (to serve)

- Hot sauce   (to serve)

Instructions:

1. Firstly, gather all ingredients.
2. Take a bowl, put the shredded veg into it, and add the vinegar, sugar, and 1 tbsp salt.
3. Now toss everything together, then set aside to pickle quickly while you prepare the rest of the sandwich.
4. Now heat oven to 180C/160C fan/gas 4. Then cut the baguette into four, and slice each piece horizontally in half.
5. Put the pieces of baguette in the oven and let it for 5minutes until lightly toasted and warm.
6. Now spread each piece with a layer of hummus, then top four pieces with the tempeh slices and pile the pickled veg on top.
7. Sprinkle over the herbs and squeeze over some hot sauce to serve.
8. Top with the other baguette pieces to make sandwiches.

Time Required:

- Preparation Time   15mins
- Cook Time   5mins
- Total Time   20mins

PAIN AU CHOCOLAT

Ingredients:

- 1 tbsp. yeast
- 1⁄2 cup milk
- 1⁄3 cup sugar
- 1 1⁄2 cups plus 2 tbsp. unsalted butter, barely softened; plus 3 tbsp. melted and cooled
- 1 tbsp. powdered milk
- 1 tbsp. kosher salt
- 4 cups flour
- 18 1/2"-wide x 3"-long bittersweet chocolate bars

- 1 egg, mixed with 1 tbsp. water, for egg wash

Instructions

1. Stir together the yeast and a cup of water 115 115 in a stand mixer bowl attached to a flour hook. Let sit for about 10 minutes. Stir in milk, sugar, 3 tbsp. Melted butter, powdered milk, and salt. Add flour. Mix on medium speed until hard dough is formed, about 5 minutes. Move to a work surface and make into a thick square. Wrap in plastic wrap and refrigerate for 2 hours.

2. Place the remaining butter on a plastic wrap. Cover with another sheet. Shape a rolling pin, pound and butter into a 6 ", " th-check square. Sit on one side. Using a rolling pin, roll the dough into 16 squares on a lightweight work surface. Open the square of butter, and place it on the dough so that the corners of the dough stick to the center point on each side of the square. Combine the corners of the dough with the butter so

that they meet in the center. Roll the dough into a 12 " x 9 " rectangle, and then roll the dough into a 12 " x 9 " rectangle like a letter and repeat the folding. Wrap in plastic wrap; Cool for 30 minutes. Repeat the rolling and folding dough twice. Cool for 1 hour.

3. Roll the dough into 20 " x 14 " x ¼ ¼ thick sheets. Cut each half in half lengthwise into about 9 triangles, about 3 3 wide at their base cut a deep-deplet slit in the middle of each wide base. Place 1 chocolate bar parallel to the base near the cut; Holding the tip of the opposite corner down, roll the base towards the base of the chocolate until it becomes a hard roll. Place the croissant on a baking sheet made of growth paper, place the tip side down, and brush with egg wash. Repeat with the remaining triangles, bars, and egg wash. Let the cruisers sit for about 2-3 hours until they double in size.

4. Heat oven 375. Working with one baking sheet at a time, brushing croissants with more egg wash; Deep golden brown, bake for about 20 minutes.

MARQUISE AU CHOCOLATE

Ingredients:

For the marquise

- 13 oz. bittersweet chocolate, chopped
- 1 stick (4 oz.) unsalted butter, cut into 16 pieces
- 4 large egg yolks, at room temperature
- 1/3 cup plus 3 Tbsp. sugar, divided
- 1/4 tsp. fleur de sel, or a pinch fine sea salt
- 1 1/4 cups cold crème fraîche
- 1/4 cup cold milk
- 12 Speculoos cookies

For the ganache (optional)

- 8 oz. semisweet or bittersweet chocolate, finely chopped
- 1 1/4 heavy cream, or more as needed

Instructions

1. Line 8-8-22 to 9 inch metal loaf pans with plastic wrap, smooth the plastic evenly around the sides of the pan and leave it open as much as possible.
2. Place a heat-proof bowl on the pot of boiling water, making sure that the water does not reach the bottom of the bowl. Add the chocolate and butter to the bowl; Heat, stir, until just melted and velvety. (Do not overcook.) Take out the cup and rest for 15 minutes at room temperature.
3. Whisk is attached to the stand mixer or handheld electric mixer is placed in a large bowl. Beat the eucalyptus, cup of sugar, and salt at medium speed until the mixture is light in color and deepened for about 2 minutes.

4. Add the yolks to the melted chocolate mixture, and mix gently using a spatula. Transfer to a separate large bowl.

5. Put the cream frame and milk in a stream mixer or bowl (you don't need to clean it first) to fit the whisper, and stir at medium speed until the mixture starts to thicken. Slowly add the remaining 3 tablespoons of sugar.

6. Pour a tablespoon of the cream frame mixture over the chocolate and mix it gently to add. Put in chopped cookies.

7. Spoon the mousse into the prepared bread pan, pushing it all the way to the corners and smoothing out the top. Cover with plastic wrap and freeze the marcos for at least 6 hours or 1 month.

8. When ready to serve, make songs: In a medium heat-proof bowl, add the chocolate. Bring the cream to a boil and pour half of it over the chocolate. Let rest for 30 seconds, then using a spatula, gently shake the chocolate and cream in small

circles. Add in the rest of the cream, or more as needed, until the ganache is smooth, shiny, and just thin enough to coat the marches without running them completely.

9. To remove the marquee, leave it in the pan. Gently tug over the plastic wrap and place it on a cooling rack set on top of the rimmed baking sheet. Cover with gauze, coat evenly and leave any extra runs on the baking sheet. Allow to set slightly, then transfer to freezer if desired. Marcos are well frozen, but are better when semi-frozen or even defrosted. Serve chopped into about 1 inch thick pieces (wet and clean the knife before each cut)

10. With a cream-framed doll, if desired.

SEAFOOD SOUP WITH GINGER AND YUZU KOSHO

Ingredients

For the broth

- 1 tbsp. olive oil
- 6 scallions, white and light green parts very thinly sliced
- 3 garlic cloves
- 1 large shallot, thinly sliced, rinsed and dried
- 1 lemongrass stalk, trimmed, tender bulb parts very thinly sliced
- One 1-inch piece fresh ginger, peeled and very thinly sliced
- 1 thin slice red chile pepper
- 1 small strip lime zest
- Salt
- 1 tsp. tsp. red yuzu kosho
- 1/4 cup dry white wine or vermouth
- 5 cups chicken, fish, or vegetable broth

- Pinch of sugar

For the fish and vegetables

- 24 mussels, scrubbed
- 1 1/2 lb. skinless cod fillet, or other firm white fish
- 24 medium shrimp, peeled and cleaned
- 6 large, head-on shrimp, or substitute peeled
- 6 scallions, white and light green parts only
- 2 large white or brown mushrooms such as cremini, trimmed and thinly sliced
- 1 shallot, very thinly sliced, rinsed in cold water and strained
- 1/2 sweet potato (cut crosswise), peeled and thinly sliced
- 1 handful baby spinach
- Salt
- Lime wedges, for serving (optional)
- Chopped cilantro or seaweed flakes, for serving (optional)

Instructions

1. Make broth: Heat oil in a large Dutch oven or pot over medium heat. Stir in the scallions, garlic, lettuce, lemongrass, ginger, chili and lime. Season with salt and cook, stirring occasionally, until soft and fragrant, about 5 minutes. Stir in yuzo kosho, then wine. Turn the heat to medium and cook, stirring, until almost steamy, 1-2 minutes. Add the prepared broth and bring to a boil. Bring to a boil, cover, and cook for 20 minutes. Add a pinch of sugar and flavor and adjust the salt. Peel a squash, grate it and squeeze the juice. The broth can be chilled for 3 days or frozen for 1 month.
2. Make fish and vegetables: Boil the broth. Reduce to a simmer and add the crumbs. Cover and cook for 3 minutes. Add the remaining ingredients and cook, uncovered, until the shrimp turn pink and the muscles open, 2 minutes (remove any spices that are not). Remove the pot from the pot.
3. Divide fish, vegetables, and broth into 6 shallow bowls. Squeeze with lime juice and

sprinkle with this cilantro or seaweed, or serve with garnish on the side.

CRÊPES SUZETTE

Ingredients:

For the Crêpes

- 6 tbsp. flour
- 6 eggs
- 6 tbsp. milk
- 3 tbsp. heavy cream
- Unsalted butter, as needed

For the Sauce

- 3 oranges
- 16 tbsp. unsalted butter, softened
- 10 tbsp. sugar
- 7 tbsp. Cointreau
- 1 tbsp. kirsch
- 1 tsp. orange flower water

- 5 tbsp. cognac

Instructions

1. Make a crepe batter: Mix the flour and eggs together in a medium bowl. Add milk and cream, and whisk until smooth. Cover with a fine strainer, cover, and refrigerate for 2 hours or overnight.

2. Prepare the sauce: Use vegetable peels to remove the rind from 2 of the oranges, avoid this. Cheema Rind and set aside. Add all the orange juice and set aside. In a medium bowl, simmer the butter and 1-2 cups of sugar on the speed of the hand mixer until light and fast, stirring for about 2 minutes. Add rind to butter and beat for 1 minute. Slowly drizzle in the juice, 2 tbsp. The water of the canteen, crunch, and orange blossoms, about 2 minutes more, is constantly beating until it is very light and fast.

3. Make croissants: Heat a seasonal crop pan or small non-stick skeleton over medium

heat until hot. Add a little butter to the green pan, then add 1 cup4 cups to the batter. While working quickly, just turn the batter over in a coat pan, and cook for about 1 minute until the edges are brown. Turn a spatula and brown on the other side for about 30 seconds. Transfer to a plate and repeat with the rest of the batter, only the greens pan as needed.

4. To serve: Melt the orange butter sauce in a 12 " skeleton over medium heat until bubbling. Dip both sides of a sauce into the sauce, then, facing down, fold in the best side, in half, then in half. Repeat the process with the remaining crops, arranging them around the pan and overheating. Sprinkle with remaining sugar. Remove the pan from the heat, place the remaining centrifuges and conic on the croup, and carefully ignite with a match. Spoon the sauce over the croup until the flame is gone, and then serve immediately.

PEAR TARTE TATIN

Ingredients:

For the Pastry

- 1 cup flour
- 1 tsp. salt
- 6 tbsp. butter, cut into small pieces
- 2 tbsp. shortening

For the Filling

- 2 lb. firm pears, peeled, cored, and halved lengthwise
- Juice of 1 lemon
- 1 1⁄4 cups sugar
- 6 tbsp. unsalted butter

Instructions

1. In a large mixing bowl, combine flour and salt, then rub butter and shortening into flour with your fingertips until it resembles coarse crumbs. Sprinkle 3 tbsp. ice water, 1

tablespoon at a time, into flour mixture, and knead until dough just holds together. Wrap dough in plastic and refrigerate.

2. Preheat oven to 425°. To fan pears, place core-side down on a cutting board. Starting from just below the stem, cut each one into 4 lengthwise slices, leaving stem end attached. Place in a bowl, gently toss with lemon juice and 1/4 cup of the sugar, and set aside for 20 minutes.

3. Meanwhile, melt butter in a 9" ovenproof skillet over medium heat. Add remaining 1 cup sugar and cook, stirring constantly, until it turns golden brown and caramelized. Remove skillet from heat. Stir to cool, as the sugar will continue to darken even off the heat.

4. Drain pears and place in skillet with caramelized sugar round side down, with stems facing center. Gently fan slices out.

5. Roll out dough on a floured work surface into a 10" round about 1/4" thick. Place dough on top of pears, covering edge of

skillet. Press edges down between pears and inside of skillet and cut four 1/4" steam holes in center. Bake for 25 minutes or until pastry is golden brown.

6. Remove skillet from oven and tilt it carefully, using a baster to draw off excess juices. Transfer juices to a small saucepan and reduce over high heat until thick. Place a large, flat serving platter on top of the skillet and invert quickly and carefully. Spoon the reduced caramelized juices over the pears. Serve warm or at room temperature.

SALMON RILLETTES

Ingredients:

- 2 scallions, white and light green parts minced (1/4 cup), dark green parts reserved
- 1 lemon
- 1/2 cup dry white wine

- Salt
- 8 oz. salmon fillet (preferably wild Alaskan), skin and bones removed
- 2 tbsp. unsalted butter, softened
- 1 small shallot, minced, rinsed, and dried Freshly ground black pepper
- 1/4 lb. smoked salmon, cut into thin strips or small squares
- 1/4 cup mayonnaise
- 2 tbsp. grainy Dijon mustard
- 1 tbsp. capers, rinsed, patted dry, and finely chopped
- 1/2 tsp. honey
- 2 tbsp. minced dill
- 1 tbsp. minced cilantro
- Crackers or sliced baguette, for serving

Instructions

1. Toss the dark scallops with a thin slice of lemon in a medium saucepan. Add alcohol, 1-2 cups of water, and a pinch of salt. Add salmon fillet to bring to a boil; Reduce to a simmer, cover, and cook for 1 minute.

Remove the pan from the heat; Set aside (covered) for 10 minutes. Transfer the salmon to a plate and refrigerate for 20 minutes or 1 day (cover if refrigerating overnight). Discard cooking liquid.

2. In a medium bowl, beat the butter with a flexible spatula until smooth. Add half a lemon juice, lemon juice, chemical scraps, bounce, a pinch of salt, and 2 pinches of pepper juice. Stir well. Stir in smoked salmon.

3. In a small bowl, combine mayonnaise, mustard, capers, honey, 1-22 teaspoons lemon juice, and a pinch of pepper. Add to the smoked salmon mixture. Stir well to collect.

4. Remove from the fridge or cooked salmon and cut into slices. Cut into pieces as much as possible, slowly stirring in the smoked salmon mixture. Taste and adjust salt, pepper and lemon juice if needed. Put chopped Delhi and grind.

5. Transfer the raisins to a serving bowl or jar. Serve immediately, or preferably cover and refrigerate for 6 hours or 3 days. Serve with chopped bags or crackers.

HONEY-AND-TEA JAMMER COOKIES

Ingredients:

- For the sablés and jam
- 1⁄3 cup cup sugar
- 1 tbsp. loose leaf green, black, or rose tea
- 9 tbsp. (4 1/2 oz.) unsalted butter, at room temperature, plus more for greasing
- 1⁄2 tsp. fine sea salt or kosher salt
- 3 tbsp. honey
- 1 tsp. pure vanilla extract
- 1 large egg yolk, at room temperature
- 2 cups all-purpose flour
- 1⁄3 cup thick strawberry jam
- For the streusel
- 3/4 cup all-purpose flour
- 3 tbsp. sugar

- 1 tbsp. brown sugar
- 1/4 tsp. cinnamon
- 1/4 tsp. fine sea salt
- 5 1/2 tbsp. (2 3/4 oz.) cold unsalted butter, finely diced
- 1/2 tsp. pure vanilla extract

Instructions

1. Make syrups: In a stand mixer or large bowl, mix sugar and tea until fragrant. Add the butter and salt, and beat using a paddle attachment, smooth over medium speed, for 3 minutes. Add honey and vanilla and beat, scrape the bowl as needed, 2 minutes. Beat in the yolk lightly. Turn off the motor, add the flour, then mix at low speed, scrape the bowl as needed, until just added.

2. Divide the dough into two and shape each half into a disc. Do one thing at a time, roll the disc between the sheets of leather and 1ich4 inches thick. Slide the dough and parchment paper on a baking sheet (you can stack them) and let cool for at least 1

hour or 2 hours. (Flour wrapped tightly in plastic wrap can be frozen for 2 months or refrigerated for 2 days.)

3. Make stews: Meanwhile, in a clean bowl of a stand mixer, or by hand, mix a little flour, sugar, cinnamon and salt. Add butter and toss in coat. Fit into the bowl with the attach attached to the bowl and mix on medium low until moist, greasy crumbs form, when pinched, about 10 minutes. Sprinkle with vanilla and mix until smooth. Cover and refrigerate for at least 1 hour but preferably 4 hours. Strocell can be stored in an airtight container in the refrigerator for up to 2 weeks or frozen for 2 months (melted in the refrigerator).

4. Center a rack in the oven and preheat to 350. Add 2 muffin tins (or use non-stick) grease. While working with one piece of flour at a time, peel off two sheets of parchment paper and place the dough on a sheet. Using a 2-inch round cookie cutter, cut the dough and place the balls in a

muffin tin. Don't worry if the dough doesn't fill the molds completely yet.

5. Place 1-2 numbers. Jam in the middle of each cookie. Sprinkle stereosyllabic around the edges (avoid covering the jam).

6. Bake, turning the tones once, until the streaks are golden brown, 20-22 minutes (jam may bubble). far off; Let the cookies rest for 15 minutes before transferring to the rack, until cool. Repeat with the remaining flour using cool tones. Cover and store at room temperature for 2 days or freeze for 2 months.

THE ULTIMATE POT ROAST

Ingredients:

- For the beef
- One 4 1/2-lb. bone-in beef shank
- Salt
- 1⁄4 cup plus 3 Tbsp. canola oil

- 10 garlic cloves, peeled
- 8 large shallots, peeled and sliced 1/2 inch thick (3 1/2 cups)
- 1/2 lb. shiitake mushrooms, stemmed and quartered (3 1/2 cups)
- 3 dried ancho chiles, halved and seeded
- 2 dried guajillo chiles, halved and seeded
- 1 bottle (750-ml) dry sauvignon blanc
- 3 cups Rich Beef Bouillon
- 2/3 cup small taggiasca or niçoise olives, drained
- Seeds and pulp of 2 passion fruits (3 Tbsp., optional)
- Flaxseed relish, for serving (optional)
- For the radishes
- 2 large bunches round red radishes (1 1/2 lb.), washed, dried, very large leaves trimmed
- 3 tbsp. olive oil

- Salt

- Freshly ground black pepper

Instructions

1. Make beef: Whole beef seasoned with beef seasoning. Use immediately or refrigerate for 1 hour, or overnight.

2. In a large (6 quart) Dutch oven or other heavy bottled, oven-proof pot, heat 1⁄4 cup canola oil over high heat. Once very hot, add the beef carefully and cook, turning as needed, until dark brown on all sides, about 20 minutes. Remove the meat to a plate and remove the fat from the pan.

3. Keep the pot on medium heat (do not clean it). Heat the remaining 3 tablespoons of canola oil over low heat. Add garlic and slots and cook, stirring frequently, until light brown and soft, about 6 minutes. Add mushrooms and dried chillies and cook

occasionally, stirring, until mushrooms are tender, about 5 minutes. Place the vegetables on a plate. Add about a third of the wine and beef shrimp to the pot. Boil over high heat. Bring to a boil, cover, and cook until the liquid has almost completely evaporated, about 20 minutes. Repeat this process twice more, adding one third of the wine bottle to the pot each time.

4. Meanwhile, preheat the oven to 325. Add the prepared vegetables, half an olive, and the mad fruit pulp to the pot. Pour into a bowl and bring to a boil, then cover the pot and transfer to the oven. Cook, taste or turn the meat and bone every 30 minutes, until the meat is pulled enough from the bone and easily cracked for 3 hours. Remove the pot from the oven. Increase the temperature to 350.

5. Remove the beef from the pot and transfer to a rimmed platter from time to time. Using a chopped spoon, remove all the solids from the brie liquid to the bowl. Leave out any large chunks of Chile that are still hard. If the sauce is not well reduced in the pot, return the pot to medium-high heat and boil the sauce until it is black. Put the rest of the vegetables back in the pot, and stir in the remaining olives. Carefully return the beef to the pot and cover to keep warm.

6. Make the radishes: On a large baking sheet, spread the radishes and greens in a single layer. Sprinkle with olive oil and season with salt and pepper, tossing and rubbing on coat. Transfer to the oven and fry until the radishes are crispy tender and the greens are peeled in 10-212 minutes.

7. Transfer the meat to a deep frying pan, and top with a spoonful of some brie liquid. Spoon the rest of the liquid and vegetables around the cow. Serve hot, chopped or sliced with a spoonful over roasted radishes and beef.

LENTIL SALAD WITH PORK BELLY

Ingredients:

- 1 small yellow onion, peeled
- 6 whole cloves
- 1 lb. puy lentils soaked overnight
- 1 lb. skinless pork belly
- 2 carrots, trimmed and peeled
- 1 rib celery
- 3 tbsp. Dijon mustard
- 3 tbsp. white wine vinegar
- 3 tbsp. finely chopped parsley
- 1 red onion, thinly sliced
- Kosher salt and freshly ground black pepper

Instructions

1. Stud the onion with cloves. In a large saucepan, cover the onion, the lentils, pork belly, carrots, and celery with 6 cups water. Bring to a boil. Reduce the heat to maintain a simmer and cook, uncovered, for 15 minutes or until the lentils are tender. Drain, discarding the onion. Finely dice the carrots and celery and cut the pork into 1/4-inch thick slices.

2. In a medium bowl, whisk the mustard and vinegar. Add in the vegetables and pork belly along with the lentils, parsley, red onion, salt, and pepper and toss to coat. Transfer to a bowl to serve.

FROMAGE BLANC CHEESE SPREAD (CERVELLE DE CANUT)

Ingredients:

- 12 oz. fromage blanc
- 1 1/2 tbsp. finely chopped chervil

- 1 1/2 tbsp. finely chopped chives
- 1 1/2 tbsp. finely chopped parsley
- 1 1/2 tbsp. finely chopped tarragon
- 2 tsp. olive oil
- 2 tsp. red wine vinegar
- 2 tsp. white wine vinegar
- 1 garlic clove, mashed into a paste
- Kosher salt and freshly ground pepper

Instructions

1. In a medium bowl, mix fromage blanc with chervil, chives, parsley, tarragon, olive oil, vinegars, garlic paste, salt, and pepper. Refrigerate until ready to serve.

MERINGUE FLOATING IN CRÈME ANGLAISE (ÎLE FLOTTANTE)

Ingredients

- 3 3/4 cups sugar
- 1/4 tsp. Preema red food color powder

- 8 oz. (2 cups) whole almonds
- 1 tbsp. orange blossom water
- 2 vanilla beans (1 scraped, 1 split)
- 3 cups milk
- 6 egg yolks
- 10 egg whites

Instructions

2. In a small saucepan, combine 2 cups sugar and red food coloring powder with 1-2 cups of water over medium heat. Using a candy thermometer, cook until the temperature reaches 118, about 18 minutes. Stir in almond, orange blossom water, and vanilla seeds; Stir until crystallized, 4 minutes. Spread the pearl rose on a baking sheet lined with parchment paper until cool.

3. Place the split vanilla bean and 2 cups of milk in a heavy bottled saucepan and bring to a simmer over medium heat. In a mixing bowl, add egg yolks and 1⁄4 cup sugar. Reduce heat and slowly stir in 1-2

cups of warm milk into the egg mixture, then add the egg mixture to the remaining hot milk. Cook, stirring constantly with a wooden spoon, until the mixture thickens, about 15 minutes. Remove from heat, strain through a fine sieve, and transfer to a bowl. Stop cooking by placing the bowl in a large bowl of ice water. Throw the vanilla bean seeds into the custard and discard the beans. Cool the Crime Ingles at room temperature, then refrigerate until cold. (Refrigerate for 3 days.)

4. In a medium saucepan, combine the remaining 1 cup of milk with 1-2 cups of sugar and 8 cups of water. Boil Reduce heat to maintain a simmer and cook for 2 minutes until sugar dissolves. Reduce heat to medium and keep warm.

5. In a large bowl and using a hand mixer, beat the egg whites on soft tops for 3 minutes. Add 1/2 cup sugar and keep beating until hard peaks are formed.

Using 2 cup measurements and working in batches, make the meringue in half a circle and dip in the milk mixture. Cook, turning as needed, until meringues are firmly set on the outside, 3 to 4 minutes. Using a chopped spoon, remove and drain on a baking sheet made of paper towels.

6. Divide the cream aniseed into 4 shallow cups and place on top with each marango. Sprinkle with preline roses.

7. In a small saucepan, heat the remaining 1-2 cups of sugar and 1 tablespoon of water over high heat, stirring occasionally, until dark amber, about 6 minutes. Quickly, and using a spoon, drizzle the caramel over the marijuana until set. Immediately Serve.

POTATO SALAD WITH HERRING

Ingredients:

- 1 lb. fingerling potatoes
- 1/4 cup finely chopped white onion
- 2 tbsp. finely chopped chives
- 2 tbsp. olive oil
- 2 tbsp. red wine vinegar
- 2 tbsp. white wine
- 2 cured herring fillets cut into 1/2-inch pieces (about 5 oz.)
- Kosher salt and freshly ground pepper

Instructions

1. In a medium saucepan, cover the potatoes with water and boil until tender, 15 minutes. Cool slightly, and then slice into 1-inch pieces.
2. Toss potatoes in a large bowl with remaining ingredients and serve warm.

LYONNAIS SALAD WITH SAUSAGE AND WALNUTS

Ingredients:

- 1 lb. saucisson pistache or mortadella, cut in 1/4-inch thick slices, then quartered
- 1/2 cup chopped toasted walnuts
- 2 tbsp. finely chopped parsley
- 2 tbsp. finely chopped shallots
- 2 tbsp. walnut oil
- 1 tbsp. white wine vinegar
- Freshly ground black pepper

Instructions

1. In a medium bowl, toss all ingredients together and transfer to a serving platter.

PIKE CAKES WITH CRAYFISH SAUCE (QUENELLES DE BROCHET)

Ingredients:

- 1 1/2 lb. skinless, boneless pike or sole, roughly chopped
- 4 large eggs, lightly beaten
- 6 cups heavy cream
- Kosher salt and freshly ground white pepper
- Cayenne
- Nutmeg
- 3 lb. 1 lb. crayfish or whole lobster, steamed
- 2 tbsp. olive oil
- 4 large button mushrooms, roughly chopped
- 2 carrots, peeled and roughly chopped
- 2 ribs celery, roughly chopped
- 1 leek, roughly chopped
- 1/4 cup tomato paste
- 2 oz. cognac

Instructions

2. In a food processor, grind the fish until smooth. Transfer to a large bowl and gently stir in the eggs. Slowly stir in 2 cups of cream, salt, pepper, red pepper, and nutmeg. Cover overnight and refrigerate.

3. The next day, separate the meat from the curry fish balls. Cut the tail into 1⁄2 inch thick slices and cook until ready to use. Heat the olive oil in a large soup pan over medium heat. Add the curryfish balls and cook, breaking them to extract the juice, for 7 to 8 minutes. Add mushrooms, carrots, celery, and leeks and cook until soft, about 10 minutes. Add tomato paste and cook for 2 minutes. Stir in the cognac and cook until the liquid has evaporated for about 1 minute. Stir in the remaining 4 cups of cream, reduce heat to maintain boiling, and cook for 20 minutes. Using a fine mesh strainer on top of a bowl, drop

the solid sauce, solid objects. Season with salt and pepper and keep warm.

4. Meanwhile, cover the work surface with plastic wrap. Place 1 cup of mousse on the edge of the plastic wrap near you, leaving a border of about 2 inches. Working with a long end and using a plastic wrap to lift and guide the muffler, roll the mouse, log. Twist the ends of the plastic wrap to secure. Wrap in plastic wrap once more and keep aside. Repeat this process with the rest of the mousse until you have four logs.

5. Bring to a simmer over medium heat. Add mousse logs and place a small saucepan or weight on them to make sure they stay submerged. Cook for about 45 minutes until set, then drain. Wait 5 minutes, then transfer to an ice bath until cool.

6. Heat oven 375. Unwrap the logs and place each in an oven-proof individual dish or in a 9-by-13-inch baking dish. Cover each with 1-2 cups of sauce and

cook for about 12 minutes until bubbling. Divide the tail pieces between each baking dish and raise the oven temperature to 425 degrees. Cook until the tops of each mousse are golden brown, 6 to 8 minutes long.

CARROT MUFFINS

This recipe is going to give you a comforting and convenient breakfast with a boost of taste and deliciousness. Take a notepad and include this recipe in a list of your favorite recipes. The beautifully vibrant colors of this recipe are going to please your eyes. You will never enjoy a better breakfast in a rush than this one.

Time required:

10 minutes, ready to serve in 30 minutes

Ingredients:

1. Almond flour – 2 cups
2. Unsweetened shredded coconut – ½ cup

3. Ground turmeric – 1 tsp
4. Baking soda ¾ tsp
5. Sea salt and ground cinnamon – ¼ tsp
6. 2 large eggs
7. Pure maple syrup – ½ cup
8. Melted coconut oil – 3 tsp
9. Pure vanilla extract – 1 tsp
10. Grated carrots – 1 ½ cups

Instructions:

11. Take a muffin tin baking sheet. Grease it with oil or cooking spray.
12. Preheat the oven to 350 degrees F.
13. Take a large bowl and mix almond flour, coconut, turmeric, baking soda, salt, and cinnamon.
14. Take another bowl and whisk eggs, maple syrup, oil, and vanilla in it. Pour this wet mixture into dry ingredients and stir until combined. Then add carrots.
15. Using a spoon, transfer this batter into the muffin cups. Bake for about 20 minutes until ready.
16. Here is your meal ready, enjoy the taste!

POMME PURÉE

Ingredients

- 4 1/2 lb. Yukon Gold potatoes, scrubbed
- 2 cups heavy cream
- 1 lb. unsalted butter, cubed and chilled
- Kosher salt and freshly ground white pepper, to taste

Instructions

1. Place potatoes in a 6-qt. saucepan and cover with water; bring to boil. Reduce heat to medium-low; cook, covered, until tender, 1–1 1/2 hours. Drain and let cool; peel. Working in batches, pass potatoes through a ricer; transfer to a bowl and keep warm. (Alternatively, use a potato masher.) Add cream to pan; bring to a simmer. Slowly whisk in butter until sauce is emulsified. Stir in potatoes, salt, and pepper.

HONEY-GLAZED ROAST PORK WITH APPLES

Ingredients

- 1 2 1/2-lb. pork loin roast, tied
- Kosher salt and freshly ground black pepper
- 2 tbsp. honey
- 4 sprigs rosemary
- 4 sprigs thyme
- 6 tbsp. unsalted butter, cubed
- 2 medium yellow onions, cut into 8 wedges each
- 2/3 cup dry apple cider
- 5 whole sweet-tart apples, such as Gala, Fuji, or Empire, cored and quartered

Instructions

2. Preheat the oven to 350. Place the pork in a large roasting pan and season with salt and pepper. Drizzle the honey over the pork, and then arrange the rosemary and thyme

on top. Sprinkle butter over the pork, then arrange the onions in the pan around the pork.

3. Put the cider in the pan and bake until you immediately insert a reading thermometer in the middle of the pork, 120 reads, about 45 minutes. Scatter and bake the apples around the pork until the apples are soft and the pork is golden brown and the instant reading thermometer reads about 45 minutes more 160 reads.

4. Remove the pan from the oven and let the pork rest for 20 minutes. Transfer the pork to a serving plate and cut into thin slices. Sprinkle roasted apples and onions around the pork and drizzle with pan juice before serving.

BAKED APPLE TERRINE WITH CALVADOS

Ingredients

- 8 tbsp. unsalted butter, plus more for greasing
- 3 lb. sweet-tart apples, such as Gala, Fuji, or Empire, peeled, cored, and cut into 1/2-inch cubes
- 1 cup plus 2 tbsp. sugar
- 2 tbsp. fresh lemon juice
- 1/4 cup calvados
- 8 large eggs
- Whipped cream, for serving

Instructions

1. In a large skillet, melt the butter over medium heat. Add two-thirds of the apples, 2-3 cups of sugar, and lemon juice, and cook occasionally, stirring, until the apples are caramel and simmer for about 30

minutes. Remove from heat, stir in kale and salt, and allow to cool.

2. Preheat the oven to 325 degrees and add 2 quints of grease. Oval baking dish with butter. In a large bowl, combine 1/3 of the sugar with the eggs and remove from the hand mixer on medium speed until the eggs are thick and yellow, about 3 to 4 minutes.

3. Scrape the scrambled eggs into the ripe apples and gently fold until smooth. Drain the mixture into the prepared dish, scatter the remaining raw apples in the dish, and cook until the eggs are set and the apples are tender for about 35 minutes.

4. Heat the broiler. Remove the baking dish from the oven, sprinkle with the remaining 2 tablespoons of sugar, and cook until the sugar is caramel for about 2 minutes. Transfer the baking dish to a rack and allow cooling completely. Serve tern with whipped cream on the side.

DEVILED EGGS WITH CRAB

Ingredients:

- 6 large eggs, plus 4 yolks
- 1/2 cup pomegranate vinegar
- 1/2 cup soy sauce
- 1 tbsp. Dijon mustard
- 2 cups peanut oil
- 3 tbsp. plus 1/2 tsp. fresh lemon juice
- Kosher salt and freshly ground black pepper
- 2 oz. jumbo lump crabmeat
- 2 1/2 tbsp. finely diced Granny Smith apple
- 2 1/2 tbsp. finely diced avocado
- 1 tbsp. finely chopped chives, plus more chive batons, to garnish

Instructions

1. Place the whole egg in a small saucepan, cover with 1 inch of water, then bring to a boil. Remove the pan from the heat, cover, and let stand for 8 minutes. Take out the eggs and transfer them to a bowl of ice

water to stop cooking. Peel a squash, grate it and squeeze the juice. Place the eucalyptus in a small cup and set aside. Place the whites in a medium bowl, and add the vinegar and soy sauce, mixing slowly. Let stand for 15 minutes, then drain and transfer to a plate.

2. Meanwhile, in a large bowl, stir the mustard until it is smooth with the raw egg yolk. While constantly whispering, gently drizzle the peanut oil into the yellow until it becomes a mixture and thickens in the mayonnaise. Stir in 3 tablespoons lemon juice and season with salt and pepper. Spoon 3-4 cups of mayonnaise into the bowl with the yellow yolk and mesh and stir until smooth. Set aside the remaining plain mayonnaise.

3. In another bowl, combine the crab meat with the apples, avocado and chives. Stir until the remaining 1/2 teaspoon lemon juice and 1 teaspoon plain mayonnaise are

evenly mixed, then season with paint de-split.

4. Spoon the shrimp mixture into the egg whites of each egg, then drop the yolk on top. Garnish each egg with some flatbreads and serve immediately.

BOILED COW'S HEAD (TÊTE DE VEAU)

Ingredients

- 1 (12-15lb.) skin-on calf head, deboned, meat cut into 2-inch pieces, tongue removed (have your butcher do this for you)
- 1 1⁄2 tbsp. Kosher salt, plus more
- 8 large carrots
- 6 ribs celery
- 4 leeks, trimmed and washed, white and green parts separated
- 3 medium yellow onions, peeled

- 3 bay leaves
- 3 sprigs thyme
- 6 whole cloves
- 1 bunch parsley, stems and leaves separated, plus 2 tsp., finely chopped
- 1 1⁄2 lb. fingerling or German butterball potatoes, peeled
- 2 hard-boiled eggs, peeled
- 1 cup mayonnaise
- 1⁄4 cup Dijon mustard
- 2 tbsp. red wine vinegar
- 1⁄4 cup chopped cornichons
- 2 tbsp. capers
- 2 tsp. finely chopped chives
- 2 tsp. finely chopped tarragon
- 1⁄4 tsp. cayenne pepper

Instructions

1. Soak the calf's brain in cold water overnight. Put the baby's head and flesh, tongue, and a teaspoon of salt in a large bowl. Cover with cold water and bring to a boil. Reduce heat to low heat and cook,

stirring any substance for 15 minutes while preparing the fish. Add 2 carrots, 1 stick of celery, 1 greens of fat, 1 onion, 1 bay, and 1 thyme and boil for 1 hour. Strain and drain the water and vegetables.

2. Add the head, flesh and tongue back to the pot and cover with fresh water and the remaining tablespoon of salt. Bring to a boil and simmer for 45 minutes, sketching any substance that rises to the top.

3. Tie the remaining 6 carrots, 5 celery of Denmark, and the lip whites in a bundle of butcher's paths. Study the remaining 2 onions with cloves and tie the remaining bay leaves with the remaining thyme and celery stems. Add vegetables to the pot. Cook for another 30 minutes, then add the potatoes. Continue cooking for another 30 minutes.

4. As the head continues to cook, pour some cooking liquid into a small pot and add the brain. Boil for 20 to 25 minutes, until then, then set aside to cool slightly.

5. When the scalp is soft, remove the pan from the heat and remove the tongue and vegetables, placing the scalp in the liquid. Peel a squash, grate it and squeeze the juice. Cut the carrots, leeks, and celery into 2-inch pieces and remove the onions and herbs. Skip the potatoes.

6. Meanwhile, remove the whites from the hard-boiled eggs and chop finely. In a medium bowl, whisk together the hard-boiled egg yolks with the mayonnaise, mustard, and red wine vinegar until thickened. In the chopped parsley, add the egg whites, carnations, capers, chives, turmeric, red pepper, salt, and pepper, stirring, and set aside.

7. In a large, shallow serving dish, arrange the vegetables on the outside, then add the scallops. Insert the tongue and place the brain in the middle. Garnish with parsley leaves and serve with garlic.

TOMATES FARCIES

Ingredients

- 10 large vine-ripe tomatoes
- Kosher salt
- 3⁄4 cup rendered duck fat or vegetable oil
- One 2-lb. bone-in lamb shoulder
- Freshly ground black pepper
- 14 oz. duck foie gras, cut into 1/2-inch cubes
- 3 confit duck legs, bones removed, meat roughly chopped
- 8 oz. chanterelle mushrooms, roughly chopped
- 2 1⁄2 oz. Parmigiano-Reggiano, finely grated
- 1⁄2 cup black truffle juice, optional
- Piment d'Espelette
- 3 cloves garlic, smashed flat
- 3 sprigs thyme
- 1 bay leaf
- 1 cup chicken stock

- 3 tbsp. plus 1 tsp. balsamic vinegar
- Juice of 1 lemon

Instructions

1. Using a pairing knife, cut each piece of tomato 1-2 inches apart and set aside. Using a melon baller or small spoon, squeeze the inside of each tomato into a bowl, being careful not to tear the skin. Sprinkle with the inner salt of the tomatoes, then turn on a rack on a baking sheet and let simmer for 1 hour.
2. Meanwhile, preheat the oven to 300. In a medium Dutch oven, heat 1-2 cups of duck fat over medium-high heat. Season the lamb shoulder with salt and pepper, then add to the pot and cook for about 12 minutes, until golden brown on all sides.
3. Transfer the pot to the oven and cook, turning the meat halfway once, until tender and falling off the bone, about 2 2 hours. Transfer the lamb to the rack and allow to cool. Divide the meat from the bone and

remove the bone and transfer to a large bowl.

4. Heat a large non-stick skeleton over high heat. Add half the foie gras and cook on one side until dark brown, about 30 seconds, frivolous. Shake the pan to make sure the folly grass doesn't stick to the bottom. Continue cooking until cooked over medium heat, about 1-22 more minutes. Using a chopped spoon, transfer the foie gras to the bowl with the lamb, remove all the fat, and return the skeleton to the heat. Repeat with the remaining foie gras, removing all but 1 cup4 of fat from the skeleton.

5. Add the duck to the skeleton and cook, stirring occasionally, until warm, about 2 minutes. Using a chopped spoon, transfer the duck to a bowl with the sheep and weeds, and return the skeleton to the heat.

6. Add the chanterelles and cook, stirring, until they release their liquid and turn golden brown, about 4 minutes. In a bowl with the duck and foie gras, scrape off the

chanterelles and any fat, and then stir in the permanganate and sulfur juice. Season to fill with salt and peat de-split.

7. Preheat the oven to 275. In a large baking dish that fits all the tomatoes easily, chop the tomatoes. Divide the filling evenly between the tomatoes, then cover each one with the top. Sprinkle the remaining 1-2 cups of duck fat around and around the tomatoes and sprinkle the garlic, thyme and itch on top. Cook until the tomatoes are soft and the filling is hot, 20 to 25 minutes.

8. Using a tablespoon or spatula, gently transfer the tomatoes to a platter. Put the stock in the baking dish, scrape off any bits stuck on the pan, then put the pan liquid, herbs and garlic in a small saucepan. Stir in the balsamic vinegar and lemon juice in the pan, bring to a boil, and cook for about 5 minutes, reducing to 1 cup3 cups. Pour the sauce into a bowl through a fine sieve, leave out the solids, and season with salt and peppermint spice to taste. Heat the

tomatoes with a tablespoon of sauce on each, as well as serve with the extra sauce.

PROVENÇAL STUFFED SQUID

Ingredients

- 12 oz. chard or spinach, chopped, about 6 cups
- Kosher salt
- 5 tbsp. extra-virgin olive oil, plus more
- 1/4 cup homemade dried bread crumbs
- 1 large onion, finely diced, about 1 1/2 cups
- Freshly ground black pepper
- 3 tbsp. chopped flat-leaf parsley
- 2 tsp. chopped thyme
- 1/2 tsp. chopped rosemary
- 4 anchovy fillets in oil, well rinsed and chopped
- 4 garlic cloves, minced
- Cheyenne pepper
- 2 tsp. finely grated lemon zest

- 1 1/2 lb. cleaned medium squid, about a dozen, tentacles and bodies separated
- 1 cup white wine
- Wild arugula leaves, for garnish
- Lemon wedges, for serving

Instructions

1. Black for four minutes in boiling salted water, then drain under running water and cool. Thoroughly dry and squeeze the chard. Sit on one side. In a small skillet, heat 1 tablespoon olive oil over medium-high heat. Add the bread crumbs and cook occasionally, tossing, until browned and toasted, for 2 to 3 minutes. Remove from the heat and allow the bread crumbs to cool.
2. Pour 3 tablespoons of olive oil into a large skillet over medium heat. Add onion, season with salt and pepper, and cook until lightly browned, about 10 minutes.
3. Add parsley, thyme, rosemary, anchovies, garlic and red pepper. Cook, stirring, for

another 2 minutes. Transfer the onion mixture to a bowl. Add cooked chard, special bread crumbs and lemon zest. Mix well with a wooden spoon. Adjust the taste and spice.

4. Rinse the squid thoroughly with cold water and dry the stomach. Using a teaspoon, fill each squid body, taking care not to overcook. Protect open areas from the top of the teeth. Seasoned with salt and pepper, seasoned with squid on both sides. Season separately with snacks and peppers.

5. Heat a large cast iron skeleton over medium-high heat for 5 minutes. Pour a tablespoon of olive oil into the skeleton, and then add the squid bodies and fry once, until light brown, about 4 minutes. Add tents around the bodies, and then add alcohol. Cover with a lid, and cook until squid bodies and tents are soft but firm, about 1 minute. Nudge and continue cooking until the alcohol is slightly reduced, about 1 minute and season with salt and

pepper. (Note: Do not crowd the squid in the pan. If necessary, use 2 skeletons or work in batches.)

6. Transfer the squid bodies and tents to a large serving platter and place the sauce on top of the spoon. Scatter the arugula around the squid and serve with lemon zest.

CPSIA information can be obtained
at www.ICGtesting.com
Printed in the USA
LVHW012046150621
690293LV00013B/1187